Written by Susannah Bradley
Illustrated by Pete Beard

HENDERSON
PUBLISHING LTD

©1996 HENDERSON PUBLISHING LTD

Introduction

People have been playing cards for so long that no one can remember how they were invented. Many of the games played today are versions of some played in foreign countries hundreds of years ago. That is why people of different nationalities can play together without too much trouble. There may sometimes be arguments about the rules, but that can happen with members of your own family!

It is easier to learn a card game by playing it than by following the instructions from a book; and to make things simpler I have referred to all players as 'him'. If you are a girl, please don't get upset!

If you are finding it difficult to understand the instructions for a game, start playing it as you read, and you will find it becomes easier.

The Cards

The standard pack of cards has 52 cards in it, and one or two jokers. These joker cards are not often used, so take them out and put them on one side while you use the rest of the pack. Keep them safe, though, in case you ever need them. The other 52 cards can be divided into four suits. These suits have signs on them which look like this:

Hearts　　　**Spades**　　　**Diamonds**　　　**Clubs**

There are 13 cards in each suit (four 13s are 52) and in a suit there are the following cards: the numbers 2 to 10, a 1, which is called the Ace, and three picture cards; the Jack, the Queen and the King.

In most games the order of importance of these cards is this:

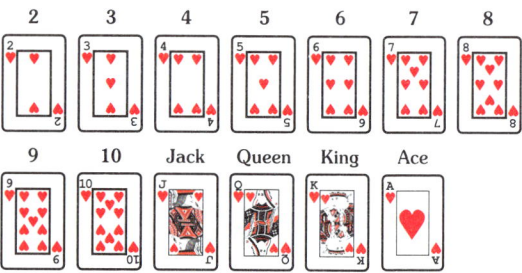

2　　3　　4　　5　　6　　7　　8

9　　10　　Jack　　Queen　　King　　Ace

2　CARD GAMES

Sometimes the Ace is 'low' which means that it is the least valuable card of all, representing 1. The instructions to every game will tell you which way the Ace should be played.

The Dealer

Every game has a Dealer who shuffles the cards and shares them out, usually one at a time and face down, to all the other players in turn. To decide who should be the Dealer, all the players take turns to cut the cards – the one who gets the card with the highest value is the Dealer. If more than one game is played, the player on the Dealer's left deals next time, and the player on *his* left deals for the third game, and so on.

Playing

Players should sit so that no one else can see which cards they hold in their hand. You mustn't tell anyone which cards you have got, because in most games a lot of the fun comes from trying to guess which cards other people are holding!

It is considered rude to pick up your cards before the Dealer has finished dealing. It might put him off, or give you an advantage by having longer to look at your cards than he does.

CARD GAMES

Card Players' Words

Card players use certain words which mean special things. Here are some of them. If you have put the pages of this book into your Funfax Organiser, you can move it along when learning a game so that these words are nearby for you to refer to.

Ace

One of four cards in each pack which may be given a value lower or higher than any other cards in the pack, depending on which game you are playing.

Cut

Cutting the cards doesn't mean attacking them with a pair of scissors – it means lifting some of the cards off the top of the pack, usually placing them under the remainder of the pack. This is done by someone other than the Dealer, to show that he hasn't been cheating.

Deal / Dealer

To deal is to share out the cards between the players. The player who does this is called the Dealer.

Deck

A set of playing cards. There are 52, and two Jokers. Another word for a deck is a pack.

Face down / Face up

Each card has a front and a back. The backs are all alike, but each card is different on the front, or face.

Hand

The cards that you are playing with – which you hold in your hand.

Pack

A complete set, or deck, of cards.

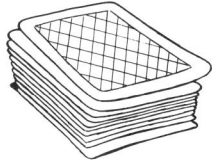

Picture card

A King, Queen or Jack.

Rank

Cards which are the same in value – for example, seven of diamonds and seven of hearts.

Shuffle

Mixing up the cards before the start of a game, so that nobody can tell what order they are in.

Suit

A set of cards, all bearing the same emblem on them. There are four suits in every pack; diamonds, clubs, hearts and spades.

Trick

The cards laid, one by each player, during a single round of certain games.

Trumps

In certain games one suit – hearts, clubs, diamonds or spades – is given special powers so that when they are used they beat all cards of the other three suits. Anyone winning by using one is said to have trumped the others.

Waste pile

Cards which have been laid during a game but not picked up by anyone.

Wild cards

Cards which can be used to represent anything you like, to help win certain games.

Games for One

Even when there is no one to play with you can still have fun with a pack of cards; there are lots of good games for one player, and we will tell you about those first.

The first two games take up lots and lots of space!

Bisley   1 player only

Take the four Aces out of the pack and shuffle the others. Then put the Aces back on top of the pack. Deal out 4 rows

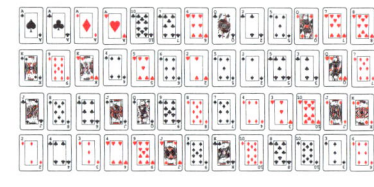

of 13 cards. As the Aces were on the top, these will be the first four cards on the top row. Look at it another way – you have 13 columns of 4 cards, the four on the left having Aces at the top.

Now you can start to move cards – but the only ones you may move are those at the bottom of a column. If you have a King at the bottom of a column you can put it above its Ace. What you have to do is build the cards in order on top of the Ace, or its King if you have got it out. You work upwards from the Ace; first the 2, then the 3, and so on – or downwards from the King – Queen, Jack, ten, and so on. But remember – you may only move the bottom card of any column!

As well as putting cards on Aces and Kings you may put the bottom card of one column on to the bottom card of another column, if it follows on in sequence either up or down. By doing this you can then get at other cards which become the bottom card of a column.

Carry on with the game until you can't move any more cards – if you're lucky you will get all the cards moved on to their Kings or Aces before that happens.

What if...?
You need to move a card which you have stacked
on another at the bottom of a column?
Move it, and the one under it too.

---

6   CARD GAMES

Paganini

1 player only

You need two packs of cards for this, and a big table (you could play on the floor if the cards are safe there from pets or baby brothers and sisters).

Shuffle the cards together – get someone to help you do this if two packs make it too much of a handful – and then deal them out in 8 rows of 13 cards. Keep the rows and columns straight or you will get into a muddle later on.

Move the Aces to the left of the display so that they make a column of their own on the left of it.

Now move into the spaces left by the Aces the cards which follow the ones on the left of each space – for example, if a 3 of hearts is on the left of a space, you put a 4 of hearts next to it. It doesn't matter what is on the right of the space.

The idea is to try to get a run of cards from Ace through to King, all of the same suit, on each row. It doesn't often happen, because the Kings sometimes catch you out! If you have a space next to one of them, the space is lost – you can't put anything into it. But one thing which helps is that you have two of everything so that you can choose which is the better of two cards to move.

What if...?
It never seems to work out?
*This game rarely does. If that bothers you,
try another game – or learn to enjoy the challenge.*

Elevens

1 player only

Many card games are adding games and this is one of them!

How To Play

Shuffle the pack and deal out nine cards, face up. These may be all in a row, in three rows of three, or in two rows with five in one and four in the other.

If any picture cards have been dealt, place another card, face up, on each of them. Then see if any other two cards add up to eleven. An Ace and a ten, for example...or a five and a six. Place a card, face up, on each of any such pairs.

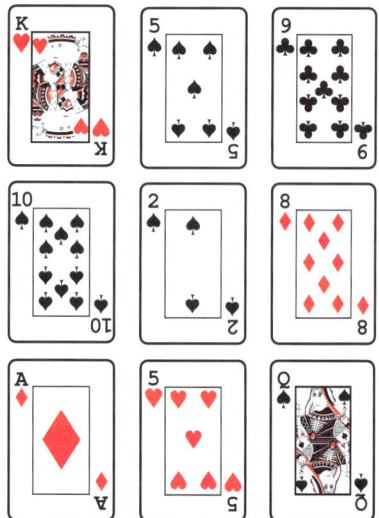

Keep doing this for as long as you can. If you can get rid of all the cards in your hand, then you've won!

What if...?
You can't remember which numbers add up to eleven?
Make yourself a check card, writing on it:
6+5, 4+7, 3+8, 2+9, and Ace+10.

Clock Patience

1 player only
This game is laid out to look like a clock, which is how it gets its name.

How To Play
Shuffle the cards and then deal out 12 cards in a circle, all face down. The first one should be at the top of the circle, where the 12 is on a clock dial, the fourth one where the three would be on a clock, the seventh where the six is, and the tenth where the nine is on a clock. Each time you make a complete round of dealing, place another card, face down, in the centre of the circle, making a 13th pile.

When all the cards have been dealt like this you will have four cards in each pile. Start by turning over the top card of the middle pile. Place it outside the circle at the number it shows on it – if it is a three, for example, put it beside the pile of cards at the 3 position, and then turn over the top card of that pile. Whatever that card is, put it outside the circle beside its number, and turn over the top card of that pile.
Aces go where the 1 would be, Jacks go beside the eleven pile, and Queens go at the top where the 12 would be. Kings go in the middle, beside the centre pile. Turning up a King is a bad thing – you hope you will get all the other cards in place before you find all the Kings.

> **What if...?**
> You get all the Kings turned over before all the other cards are face up?
> *It's the end of the game and you've lost!*

CARD GAMES

Patience

1 player only

This is said to be the hardest game of cards for one player, but it is so well-known that its name is often used for all the one player games!

How To Play

Shuffle the pack and deal out a row of seven cards, the first one face up but the others face down.
Next, deal one face up card on to the first face down card in the row, and five more face down cards to complete the row.

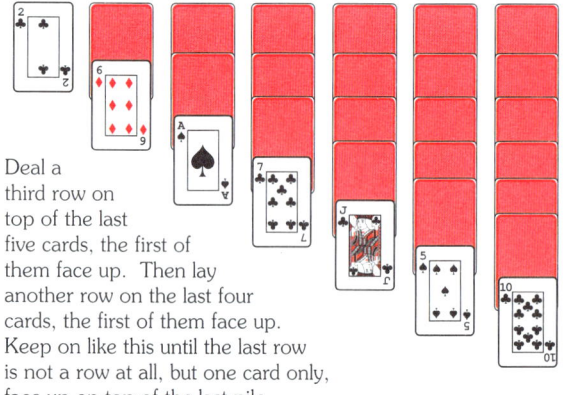

Deal a third row on top of the last five cards, the first of them face up. Then lay another row on the last four cards, the first of them face up. Keep on like this until the last row is not a row at all, but one card only, face up on top of the last pile.
Now you can start to move the cards. If there are any Aces, move them to one side, out of the game but where you can see them. Turn over the next card in the pile so that you still have a row of seven cards, face up. Remove any more Aces which show, and turn over the cards they have hidden.
Now put cards in sequence wherever possible – moving a lower card to sit on, but overlapping, any card which is one number higher and the opposite colour. In this way you get runs from King, Queen, Jack, ten, right down to two. They must always go red, black, red, black, or black, red, black, red, and so on.

10   CARD GAMES

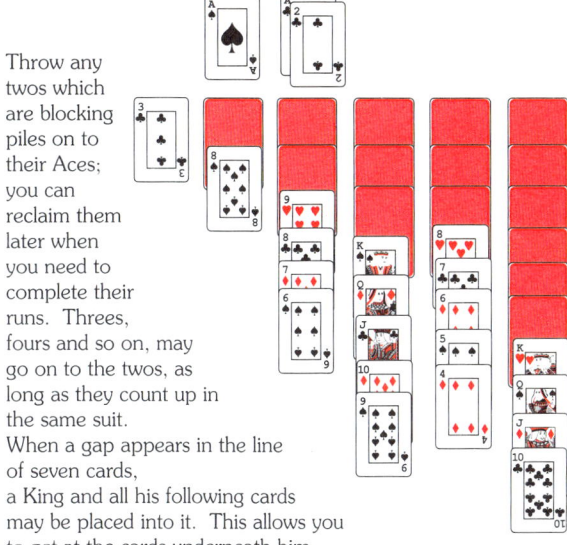

Throw any twos which are blocking piles on to their Aces; you can reclaim them later when you need to complete their runs. Threes, fours and so on, may go on to the twos, as long as they count up in the same suit.

When a gap appears in the line of seven cards, a King and all his following cards may be placed into it. This allows you to get at the cards underneath him.

When there are no more cards you can move, take the undealt part of the pack, face down, and count off three cards. Place them face up on the table. If the top one of the three can be placed in sequence, use it, and move any other cards one number lower and the other colour on to it if you can. Keep dealing on to the waste pile in threes, using each third card if you can. But don't cheat and use any other card than the top one, or the one which becomes the top one after you've moved the previous top card.

If you can get all four sequences out in lines leading from the Kings you have won – and you are very lucky, because it doesn't often happen!

What if...?
You get to the end of the waste pile without it making much difference?
Some people say that you can shuffle the waste pile and start again – but only twice after the pack has been laid the first time. In a game for one player it doesn't really matter what rules you use as long as you stick to the ones you decide on.

Shout!

1 player only

This is a good game if you are on your own as it doesn't matter how much noise you make. Actually, it's quite hard to shout out the name of one card while you are laying another, so you will have to concentrate.

How To Play

Shuffle the cards and take off the top card, shouting "Ace!" as you lay it down. Then shout "two" as you put down the second card, "three" as you lay the next, and so on up to King. Every time the card you put down is what you've shouted, put it aside. Some people believe that you can only have a limited amount of goes to get the game out, or you lose, but it's much more fun to see how many times you have to go through the pack before you get rid of all the cards. Keep a check on it and try to beat your previous best.

What if...?
You can't ever get them out?
Give up. You're out to have fun, that's all.

---

12 CARD GAMES

Move It Up

1 player only

This game goes on and on...you might have to leave it and come back to it later! It is also very hard to get out, but it's marvellous when you do.

How To Play

Shuffle the cards and deal four in a row, face up. If any of the cards are of the same value, move the last one you dealt on to the first one you dealt. If you get three cards the same at this stage, then you didn't shuffle them very well and really, you ought to start again, beginning with a good shuffle!

  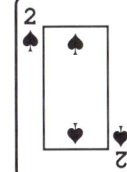 

Continue to deal four cards at a time, moving cards of the same value to the left at the end of each deal. If by doing this you reveal one from a previous round which matches one to the left of it, move that too; and if it matches one to the right of it, move the one on the right to the newly-revealed card.

When you have dealt out all the pack, pick up the piles and start again. You should pick them up in order so that the first pile is on top of the stack, the second next, and so on. Any set of four cards of the same value which appear in one dealing are taken from the piles and discarded. It can be really maddening to see the first of a set of four appearing as the last card of a deal is laid, with the other three in the next hand! But if you go on for long enough you should get it out.

What if...?
It goes on and on for so long that you have to leave it overnight?
Time it, and see if you can set a record.

Partners

1 player only

This game is very easy and quick to play. You need 32 of the cards in your pack – the easiest way is to leave out all the twos, threes, fours, fives and sixes. Be sure to put them back afterwards, won't you!

How To Play

Shuffle the cards and deal them face down in piles of four in front of you. Then turn each pile over so that you can see the top card of each one.

Now see if you can find a partner for each card (that is, one of the same value). You mustn't use any of the cards which are underneath – only the top ones. Take these partners off and start a waste pile with them.

Keep on taking partners like this for as long as you can – if you are lucky you will win the game by putting all the cards on the waste pile with their partners.

> **What if...?**
> It doesn't work out?
> *Count the number of cards on your waste pile and call it your personal best – then see if you can beat it next time.*

14 CARD GAMES

Five Fives

1 player only

What are five fives? Twenty five – and that's how many cards you need to play this game.

How To Play

Shuffle the entire pack and then count off the first twenty five cards, putting the others aside.

Next, start to make five rows of five cards – your aim is not to have two of any one value (tens, Kings, etc) in any row, be it across or down.

You may put each card down in any place you like, but once you have let go of it you may not pick it up again. This seems easy at first but if you are unlucky enough to have two of the same value when you are nearly out of cards you'll find it can be impossible!

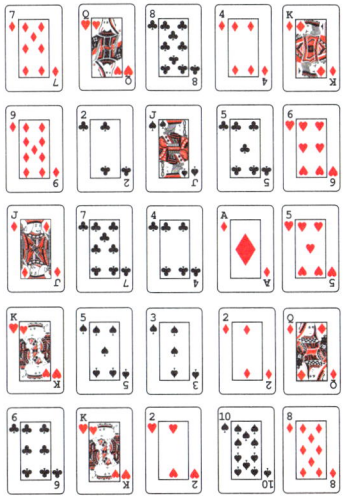

What if...?
You see that you've made a mistake as the card leaves your fingers – surely you can pick it up then?
No!

Sir Tommy

1 player only

This is a very old game but it is very hard to win – it rarely comes out, but it can be fun seeing if you can get further than you did in the game before.

How To Play

Shuffle the cards, then deal the top card. If it's an Ace you are lucky – place it face up on the table some distance from you. If it isn't an Ace, place it in front of you and deal the next three cards beside it to make a row of four. Any Ace which appears should be put out of the row, and any two, whatever the suit, should be placed on top of an Ace. Turn over the top card of those in your hand and place it on one of the piles. Which one you choose is up to you. You can have lots of cards in one pile and very few in the others if you like. What you are trying to do is to add cards in numerical order to the Aces, starting with a two, then a three, and so on up to King, on each one. To do this you have to use only the top cards of your four piles.

You may go through the pack once only – you aren't allowed to pick up your four piles and start to deal them out again. That's what makes it so difficult!

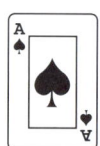
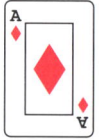

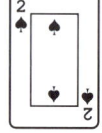

What if...?
You have a four, a Jack, an eight and a nine on your four piles, and the next card is a ten? Which pile should you put it on?
You should put it on the Jack, because you will need a ten before you need a Jack.

Apple Tree

1 player only

Shuffle the pack (this is your apple tree). Deal six cards face down in a row (these are the windfall apples which have landed in the grass). Now you have to try to pick up all the apples (that means all the cards in the pack) – and here's how you try to do it...

How To Play

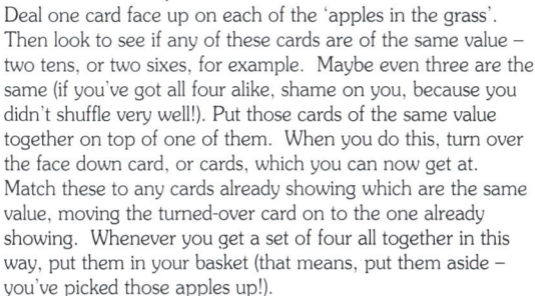

Deal one card face up on each of the 'apples in the grass'. Then look to see if any of these cards are of the same value – two tens, or two sixes, for example. Maybe even three are the same (if you've got all four alike, shame on you, because you didn't shuffle very well!). Put those cards of the same value together on top of one of them. When you do this, turn over the face down card, or cards, which you can now get at. Match these to any cards already showing which are the same value, moving the turned-over card on to the one already showing. Whenever you get a set of four all together in this way, put them in your basket (that means, put them aside – you've picked those apples up!).

Now take the undealt part of the pack and place the first three cards from it in a pile on the table. If the top card of these three cards matches one on one of your piles, add it to that pile. If the next card down can be matched too, add it to the right pile, and do the same with the third one if possible, too. Then deal three more cards in the same way, and carry on playing like this. Whenever you cannot match a card, use the next one to fill any space in your six rows which occur through moving the 'apple in the grass' at the bottom of the pile. Whenever you get a set of four in a pile together, put them in the basket. When you have dealt all the cards in groups of three, pick up those you couldn't use, turn them over and deal them out in threes again.

You've won the game when all the apples are picked and in your basket. But it doesn't always work out. Sometimes the card you need is trapped face down under the cards on top of it.

What if...?
You shuffle the cards in your hand when you have picked them up after laying them down in threes?
It won't make any difference!

CARD GAMES

Games for Two

Some of the games in the final section can be played with two players, too – but they're in the 'Three or More' section because they work well with lots of players. If you use up all the games in this section, hunt through the rest of the book.

Beggar Your Neighbour   2 players only

This is an old favourite but is lots of fun, and it doesn't take long to learn, either. Another name for it is 'Strip Jack Naked' which is really embarrassing for anyone who happens to be called Jack.

Each player has exactly half the pack (that's 26 cards each, right?) and they don't look at their cards.

How To Play

The first player puts down a card, and then the other player puts down a card on top of it, and so on. BUT...

If an Ace or a picture card is put down, the other player must top it with a picture card, or an Ace. To do this he has extra turns.

If an Ace was played, he can have four turns – but if by the fourth card he still hasn't laid a picture card or another Ace, the player who laid the first Ace scoops up all the cards laid so far and adds them to the bottom of his own pile. If a King was played, the other player has three chances before his opponent scoops them up. If a Queen was played, the other player has two chances, and if a Jack was played, the other player has only one chance.

If one of these turns produces a picture card or an Ace, then the first player has extra turns in the same way.

The winner is the player who ends up with all the cards.

What if...?
You run out of cards while you are trying to put four on an Ace?
Tough – you lose!

Heartless

2 players only

This isn't called Heartless because people have to be particularly cruel to play it, but simply because you take all the hearts out of the pack before you start – they aren't needed. This game could be played by three players, but then you would have to give all the hearts to the third player to play with and think of a new name to call the game. Actually, we have heard of it being called Gops, but goodness knows why. Diamond Mines would be a good name for it, but we haven't heard of anyone calling it that.

How To Play

There is no skill attached to this game – it is purely a matter of chance. Sort out the pack so that all the diamonds are in one pile, and one player has all the spades while the other has the clubs. Shuffle the diamonds and put them face down in a pile between you. Turn over the top diamond.

Each player then takes the top card from his hand and lays it face down on the table in front of him. Together, they turn over these cards and the person who has played the highest card wins the diamond. In this game, Ace is low (that means it only counts as 1) and the King is the highest card in the game.

Another diamond from the pile on the table is then turned over and the players play again. This goes on until all the diamonds have been bid for. To find out who has won, each player must add up the value of the diamonds he has won. The King of diamonds counts for 13 points, the Queen 12 and the Jack 11. All the others are worth the number they show. The game may be carried over into further rounds, adding the totals scored to previous totals.

What if...?
Both players play cards of the same value at once?
The diamond they are playing for stays on the table and the next player to win a card takes that one too.

CARD GAMES

Gin Rummy

2 players only

This is just one of several games in the Rummy family, and it is the best kind of Rummy for two players – although it can be adapted to allow three, or even four people to play.

How To Play

The Dealer deals 10 cards to each player, one at a time, and then puts the rest of the pack, face down, on the table. He turns over the top card and places it next to the pile. The purpose of this game is to collect groups of cards which go together – three (or even four) sevens for instance, or Kings, or anything else – or which follow in sequence in the same suit, such as the eight, nine, ten and Jack of clubs, say. The best hand of all to have is one in which all the cards belong to a group of three or more. When this happens you are said to have a 'gin' – and you win!

Each player's chance to improve his hand comes when it is his turn. Then he can exchange one of his cards for either the waste card, or for one which no one has seen on the top of the pile. Taking the waste card means that you know what you are getting, but the disadvantage is that the other players know what you are collecting, and will think "Ha ha! If he's collecting fours, I'd better not throw any away! Or it might be a run, so I won't throw that three out either!".

There are two ways to end a game of Gin Rummy. The first way is the best – you go out as soon as you can place all your cards on the table in sets. Your opponent has to count up the value of any cards he holds which are not in sets.

Picture cards score 10 points, Aces score 1, and everything else scores its face value. The winner scores 25 points for getting a gin and he also scores the value of his opponent's leftover cards too.

The other way to end the game is to call "knock" just before you lay a card on the waste pile (having just picked one up). All cards don't have to be in sets, but those which aren't mustn't add up to more than 10.

Then both of you lay your cards on the table, whether they are in sets or not. And because you called "Knock!" he can add unmatched cards of his own on to yours – for example, if you have three Queens he can add another, or he could add a three and a seven of hearts to your run of four, five and six of hearts.

When that's been done he adds up the value of his remaining cards. If it comes to more than the ones you have left, it is known as a successful 'knock' and you score the difference between your penalty points and his. But if his points are less, he gets 25 bonus points plus the penalty points difference between you.

The first player to reach 100 points wins.

> **What if…?**
> The other player gets to a score of 100 before you get any points at all?
> *The other player scores another 100 points – which is a big advantage if you are having a Rummy Championship in the school holidays!*

Oklahoma Gin

2 players only

This is nearly the same as Gin Rummy but there is one difference.

How To Play

Deal the cards and play as described in Gin Rummy. But note which card is the first one on the waste pile. If a player decided to 'knock' to go out, he mustn't have more points in his hand than the value of this first card. For instance, if it is the ten of spades, you can't 'knock' if you're going to be left with cards which add up to more than ten points. Picture cards count as ten each, too, but everything else from two upwards counts as face value.

What if...?
The first card laid was an Ace?
*You can't 'knock' – you have to go out with a gin
(all your cards have to be in sets or runs).*

Snap!

2 players or more

This is one of the best-known card games of all time, but that doesn't mean that it should be left out.

How To Play

Shuffle and deal the cards so that each player has half the pack. Now the first player puts a card down, face up, to start a waste pile. The other player places a card on top of it. If it is the same value as the card previously laid, the players have to shout "Snap!". The first one to do this picks up the waste pile. Of course, it usually isn't the same first time, but the players keep on putting cards down alternately until this happens.

The winner is the player who ends up with all the cards. This game gets very noisy because people think that by shouting loudly the other player may think they shouted first.

What if...?
You can't agree who said "Snap!" first?
Leave the waste pile alone and carry on –
it's not worth falling out over it.

CARD GAMES 23

Slam

2 players only

This is a great game that's fast and furious – and the cards sometimes get bent, so play it with old ones. Play with friends who can slam the cards down as fast as you can, instead of little brothers or sisters – or parents! – who might get upset when they can't keep up.

How To Play

Deal all the cards out so that each player has half a pack each.

Make 5 piles of cards face down in front of you, dealing in rows. The first pile has one card in it, the second has 2, the third 3, the fourth 4 and the fifth 5. Turn over the top card on each pile and put any cards of the same value together (Kings on top of Kings, etc). The other player does the same.

Each time you move a card, turn the next one face up and move it if you can. If you are lucky you will get all, or nearly all, of your cards exposed in this way – if you have less than five piles you can move a card into a gap to get at the cards trapped under it – but you are never allowed more than five piles.

Put your spare cards down between the two rows of cards and, together, turn over the top one to begin a waste pile, like this:

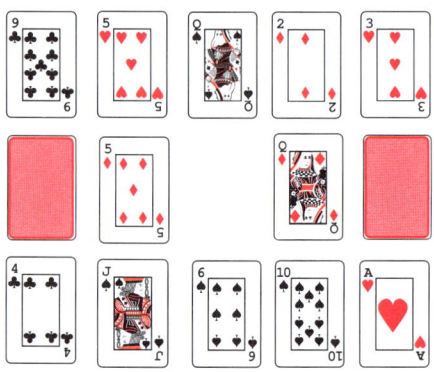

(This is the game so far.)

Now for the slamming bit!
Slam down on either discarded pile, a card from your five piles which is one place higher or lower than the card on the waste pile – for example, a six or eight on a seven. Keep doing this to whichever card is on top of your own waste pile, until neither of you can go. At the same time you have to turn over any face down cards on your piles as they become free. Sounds simple – but it's a race to slam your cards down before the other player does!

When neither of you can go, you turn over another card from each spare stack on to its waste pile. Do it at the same time, remember! Then off you go again.

When a player uses up all the cards in front of him he slams his hand over the pile with the least cards on it, thus claiming them for the next round. His opponent has to pick up the other pile, as well as all the cards he's still got in front of him (both players take their own stack of spare cards too) and they start again. It can go on for several rounds before anyone wins – and that happens by getting rid of all your cards.

> ### What if...?
> You take the bigger pile by mistake?
> *You're stuck with it!*

CARD GAMES

Slapjack

2 players only
Use old cards for this game, too – not your best ones!

How To Play
The cards are shuffled and dealt out so that each player has half the pack, placed in a stack face down in front of him. Then the player who didn't deal takes a card from his stack and lays it face up to start a waste pile exactly halfway between the two players. When he does this he must turn the card over away from himself, so that he can't sneak a look at the cards before the other person does. The other player then does the same and they take it in turns to lay cards, one on top of another, until someone puts down a Jack.

As soon as this happens the players have to slap one of their hands on top of the Jack. The one whose hand gets there first wins all the cards in the pile, and puts them face down under the cards in his stack.

Each player must use one hand for playing the cards, and the other for slapping; and anyone who slaps a card which isn't a Jack has to give one card to the other player. To stop people playing with their slapping hands hovering over the table, try making them put them on their heads.

The player who wins all the cards is the winner of the game.

What if...?
One player runs out of cards while there are still some on the waste pile?
They've lost!

Pairs

Even small children can play this, because it doesn't get any easier as you grow up!

How To Play

Use the complete pack. Shuffle the cards and spread them out, face down, on a large table or on the floor, so that no card is touching another one.
Now take it in turns to turn over any two cards of your choice. If they are the same (two Jacks, or two threes, for instance) remove them and keep them by your side. Then you may have another turn. If they are not the same you must turn them over again, putting them back exactly where they were before, and the other player has a turn. The winner is the player who ends up with the most pairs.

What if...?
A player puts a card back in a different place from the one it was in when he picked it up?
His opponent may challenge him and force him to put it back in its original place.

Games for Three or More

Games which need three players are also suitable for four or even more players. There's no upper limit, unless you don't have enough cards to go round, when sometimes you can use extra packs. Try them and see.

Snip, Snap, Snorem

This game is about 200 years old, and has lasted in many different forms. If you've been playing a different version to the one described here, just choose the one which suits you best!

How To Play

The Dealer shuffles the pack and deals the entire pack, face down and one at a time, to all the players. Then the player on the Dealer's left lays a card – any card he likes – face upwards. The next player has to put down one of the other three cards of that value, if he has one. As he does so, he says "Snip!". If he has two of the three cards he puts them both down, saying "Snip, Snap!" and if he has all three he puts them all down, saying "Snip, Snap, Snorem!".

If he hasn't any of the three cards he says "Pass", and the next player in turn has a go. The player to place the last – and say "Snorem" – gets to choose which card to put down next.

If you have two cards of the same value you have to put them down together when it is your turn, unless you are starting the round, when you may keep the second one until it is your turn again. Otherwise you put them both down and say "Snip, Snap!" or "Snap, Snorem!".

The player who gets rid of all his cards first is the winner.

What if...?
You have all four cards in your hand?
You may discard them at the start of the game.

---

28 CARD GAMES

Top That

Best with lots of players (but it can be played with 2 or 3)

Twos and tens are special in this game!

How To Play

The Dealer shuffles the cards and then deals three cards, face down, in a row, to each player, and then three more face up on top of the first three. He deals three more cards, face up, to each player, which the players pick up. The rest of the cards are placed in a stack, face down, in the centre of the table.

Before play begins, everyone looks at their cards and those which they can see on the table. If they have any low cards on the table they may swap them for other cards in their hand – picture cards or Aces (which are high) are best put on the table as they are often needed more towards the end of the game, when these cards are used. When everyone is ready, play can begin.

The player to the Dealer's left starts play by putting down a card from his hand to start a waste pile, and picking up another from the stack to replace it. He may lay any card, but it is best to save twos and tens as these have special powers; it is a good idea to get rid of low cards such as threes and fours. If he has two or three cards of the same value he may get rid of them both, or all, at once – but while there is a stack of cards on the table he must replace them by picking up more so that he always has three cards in his hand.

The next player must lay a card on the waste pile of the same value, or higher, than the one laid, and then pick up another from the stack. Any player, when it is his turn, may lay one, two or three cards of the same value, but while there are cards in the stack he must replace them. If a player has no equal or higher card to lay, he may put down a two to start a new run. If he hasn't got one and so cannot go at all, he must pick up all the cards on the waste pile. When this happens he must sort through them. He can then throw out any set of four which are the same – and by putting down two or three cards at once on his turn, he soon gets rid of them!

Ten is special because whenever one is laid, the waste pile is thrown out and a new one is started. When the stack has been used up and a player has no more cards in his hand, he may choose to play one of his three upturned cards on the table. When these have been played, he must play one of the last face down cards without looking at it first, until all the cards have been used up. Of course, his chances of winning the waste pile during this part of the game are high, but if he can get rid of all his cards without doing so, he's won the game.

What if...?
There are only two of you who want to play this game?
Deal six cards for each hand instead of three.

Go Boom

This is a popular game, well-known in most places, but no one seems to know how it got its name. In some places it is known as Rockaway.

How To Play

The Dealer shuffles the pack and then deals 8 cards face down to each of the three players. If four people play, 7 cards are dealt to each, and if there are five players, 6 cards are dealt. The rest of the pack is placed face down in the centre of the table.

The player on the Dealer's left starts play by placing any card he chooses from his hand, face up, on the table. All the other players have to do the same, in turn, but their cards must be either the same suit or the same value as the one laid. Let's say the King of spades is the first card laid. Everyone else must lay either a King or a spade. If they can't do this because they haven't got such a card in their hand, they must pick up a card from the central stack – and go on picking up one card at a time until they get a King or a spade. They can then put it down, straight away.

When everyone has played a card, the person who put down the card of the highest value wins. Ace has the highest value in this game; then comes King, Queen, Jack, and so on.

If there are two cards of the same highest value, the person who played the first one wins. The winner then turns all these cards face down, to show that they are finished with, and begins a new round, choosing whatever card he likes to begin the game again.

The winner is the first player to get rid of all his cards.

What if...?
You can't go, but there aren't any cards
left in the stack to pick up?
You have to miss a turn.

CARD GAMES 31

Joker Go Boom

This is just another way of playing which you might like to try when you've played **Go Boom** for a while.

How To Play

Add two jokers to the pack – or up to four if you can borrow a couple from another pack. Whenever you get one of these in your hand you can use it when otherwise you would have to draw from the stack; you can play it whenever you haven't got a card of the right suit or value to play...but you can't win a trick with it.

Go Fish

3 – 6 players

It is said that a game like this was played in Italy as early as 1585. If you already like playing **Happy Families** you should like this game because it is based on the same idea.

How To Play

The Dealer shuffles the pack and then deals 5 cards, face down, to each player. He then places the rest of the cards, face down, in the centre of the table. The idea of the game is to keep collecting sets of four cards. The person with the most sets at the end, wins.

Play begins with the player on the Dealer's left asking another player of his choice for a named card – let's say he asks for the seven of diamonds. He must only ask for this if he already has a seven of something else in his hand. If the person he asks has the card asked for, he has to hand it over; if not, he says "Go Fish!" and the player who asked for the card must pick one up from the stack. If the player 'fished' successfully, he can then ask that same person or another player, for another card. Play continues round the table in order, with each person choosing who they like to ask for the cards they want.

If you ask for a card from another player you must have one of the same rank already in your hand; and if you are asked for a card which you possess you must hand it over. If you are told to "Go Fish!" but there is no stack left, you just wait your turn instead.

When you have collected all four cards of the same value in your hand, you put them down in front of you.

What if...?
You pick up a card which someone asked you for earlier in the game?
If you can remember who asked you for it you know where to find at least one other of the same value, don't you!

CARD GAMES 33

Old Maid

3 – 10 players

If you have more than six players, you will need to use two packs of cards for this game, which has given a lot of fun to a lot of people since Victorian times.

How To Play

Before you shuffle the pack at the start of play, remove the Queen of spades from the pack, or from just one of the packs, if you are using two packs of cards. Shuffle the cards and deal them all out face down, one at a time, around the table. It doesn't matter if some players end up with one more card than others.

When all the cards have been dealt out everyone picks their cards up and looks at them, sorting them into pairs. A pair in this game is two of any value – they don't have to both

be red or black, but they do have to be of the same value – the two of clubs can be paired with the two of hearts, for example, even though one is red and the other black. Whenever you make a pair you put it face down in front of you on the table.

When every player has finished pairing up his cards he spreads out the cards in his hand and offers them, face down, to the player on his left, who chooses one of them. At the same time he has to take one from the hand of the player on his right. He can't see which card he is taking, but once it is in his hand he can see if another pair can be made and put face down on the table. If so, that's what he does.

Then, when everyone is ready, the cards are offered to the player on each person's left as before, and another one chosen at random.

34   CARD GAMES

When a player uses up all his cards by pairing them, he drops out of the game. At last there is only one player left, holding one card – one of the Queens, which can't be paired up because the Queen of spades has been removed. Then everyone laughs and calls him an 'Old Maid'! He has to pay a forfeit, which may be to sing a song or do whatever silly thing the others decide on.

What if...?
You know you've put one pair of Queens face down in front of you, but then you pick up the third one from your neighbour's hand? What's to stop you putting it down on the table with something else to make it into a pair?
It's cheating – and you'll be found out in the end because there will be a card left over which should have partnered the one you put down with the Queen!

Pontoon

3 – 10 players

This is also known as Blackjack, Twenty one, or Vingt et un (which is French for twenty one). As well as the pack of cards, you'll need some spent matchsticks (or buttons) if you want to bet on the game; but it's quite a lot of fun without bothering to bet. The only skill you need is being able to add up to 21!

How To Play

In this game the Aces count as either one or eleven. All the tens, Jacks, Queens and Kings count as ten each, and everything else counts as face value.

First of all choose the Dealer, and decide how many rounds he will deal for. After he has dealt for that number of rounds, choose another Dealer and give him the same amount of rounds to deal. Go on this way until you've run out of time, Dealers or matchsticks, or until you want to do something else. Everyone should have a large stock of spent matchsticks, because when they are Dealer they will have to pay out to people who win.

The Dealer shuffles all the cards and deals one card, face down, to each player including himself. Each player, except the Dealer, looks at his card, decides if it is a good or a bad card, and puts it back on the table, placing matchsticks on it. If a player thinks he's been dealt a poor card, he only puts one matchstick on it, but if he thinks it's a good one he can put more on it; the players should decide before the game starts the most matchsticks this may be.

Then the Dealer deals a second card to each player (including himself). Once more, everyone except the Dealer looks at the card; and this is where the adding-up happens. Your cards must not add up to more than 21, but they should add up to as near 21 as possible.

Anyone who is lucky enough to have cards which add up to 21 has a pontoon without doing anything! He must declare it at this point by turning over the Ace (because the only way you can get a pontoon with two cards is by having a ten or a picture card, and an Ace). The Dealer then knows that he has to equal it to win.

The Dealer then asks each of the other players in turn, "Stick, buy or twist?".

36 CARD GAMES

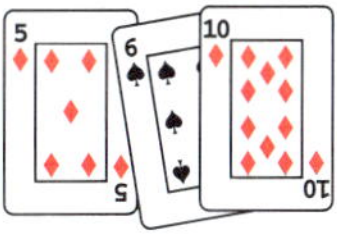

The player chooses what he wants to do. If he chooses to stick, the Dealer does not give him any more cards. To stick, a player's two cards must add up to at least 16.

If he chooses to buy, he puts down another matchstick, and the Dealer passes him a card, face down.

If he chooses to twist, the Dealer deals him a card, face up, without him having to add another matchstick to his stake. Each player may continue to buy or twist cards until he either sticks, or goes over 21. Going over 21 means that he has bust and he has to say "Bust!" and pass his cards back to the Dealer, who puts them at the bottom of the pack. The Dealer wins the matchsticks, too!

Anyone who sticks does not have to show the Dealer his cards until the end of the game.

When all the players have either bust or decided to stick, the Dealer turns his own two cards face up and counts them up. If he likes, he may deal himself more cards until he reaches 21, or as near to 21 as he dare go. Sometimes, by doing this, he will bust. If he busts, he keeps the matchsticks of those who also bust, but pays any player who scores between 16 and 21 the same amount of matchsticks as they had placed on their cards. If any of these players scored a pontoon (21 with only 2 cards) he has to pay them twice as many matchsticks as they had staked.

If the Dealer scores 21 on three or more cards, he wins everyone's stakes, except those players who scored a pontoon. As before, he has to pay them twice as many matchsticks as they had staked.

If he stops dealing cards to himself after he reaches 16 but before he gets to 21, he keeps the stakes of any player scoring the same or less than him, but has to pay the same number as staked to anyone scoring more (double to a pontoon).

What if...?
The other players don't want the Dealer to know that they have, say, a score of 21 with 3 or more cards?
They mustn't get excited about their chance of winning before the Dealer has decided to stop dealing cards to himself – players need only turn over their cards after the Dealer has decided to stick, and if the Dealer doesn't know that a player has got 21, he may stick at 19 or 20, or even less.

Cheat

3 or 4 players; up to six if you use two packs of cards shuffled together.

This is a great game for people who are excellent at telling lies!

How To Play

Shuffle the cards and have the Dealer deal three cards at a time, face down, to each player. When the whole pack has been dealt out all round in this way, and everyone has had a good look at their cards, the player on the Dealer's left places 2, 3 or 4 cards face down in the middle of the table, saying something like: "Two tens!" or "Three sevens!" or "Four Aces!".

Who knows if he's telling the truth or not? Someone may now call out, "Cheat!".

The cards are turned over and, if they are not what they were claimed to be, the cheat has to pick them up again. But if they really are what they were said to be, the accuser has to take them instead. Cards placed down must be of either the same value, or one higher or lower, than the one laid by the previous player.

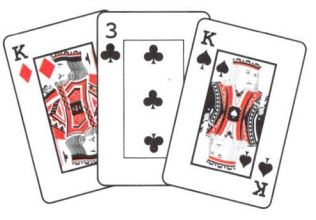

As the game goes on and the pile gets higher, it becomes really dangerous to accuse anyone else of being a cheat, because there are so many cards to be picked up! And, of course, the idea is to get rid of all your cards, not to pick lots up.

This is a game which can get very noisy and is lots of fun without being too difficult for smaller children to understand, so it is a good family game.

What if...?
You want to lay down 2 cards when
the previous players have put down four?
*You can put down however many you like,
between 2 and 4, when it is your turn.*

---

38   CARD GAMES

Pishti

This game is thought to be Turkish, but there is a Greek version, too. It's known as a fishing game – you'll see why when you learn it.

How To Play

The Dealer shuffles the pack and deals 4 cards to each player and 4 to a pile in the centre of the table. No one looks at the cards dealt to him (and certainly not at anyone else's!). When the Dealer has finished dealing he turns over the top card of the middle pile.

Each player in turn, starting with the player on the Dealer's left, turns over his own top card and places it on the pile; if it is the same value (not suit) of the one already on the top, he wins all the cards on the pile. The next player then has to start a new pile, playing their top card.

When all the cards the players hold have been used, another round of four cards is dealt and played, and so on, until there are no more cards left.

That's all there is to it – and if you think that's not enough to make an interesting game, you can keep a score as you go along. Here are the scoring rules:

Anyone winning a 'pile' which has only one card on it is said to have scored a 'pishti' – 10 points.

At the end of the game other points are awarded:

- the player with the most cards gets 3 points
- the player with the ten of diamonds scores 3 points
- the player with the two of clubs gets 2 points
- for having an Ace – 1 point (a point for each Ace)
- 1 point for every Jack

What if...?
You want to liven it up a bit more?
Some people play the bluffing rule. When a pile contains only one card, the next player to lay a card may place it face down and claim a 'pishti'. If no one challenges him, he wins the card and scores 10, but if someone accuses him of cheating he has to turn it over; if it really is a 'pishti' he scores 20 instead of 10 for it, but if he was cheating the person who challenged him gets 20 points instead.

CARD GAMES 39

Decisions

You have to think fast in this game because there are decisions to be made all the time!

How To Play

In this game, Kings have no value, Aces count as 1, Jacks and Queens score 10, and everything else is worth its face value. The idea is to score as little as possible in this game – so Kings and Aces are the cards to get!

The Dealer shuffles the cards and deals four face down to each player, placing the remainder in a pile in the centre of the table.

Then everyone arranges his cards in two rows of two, like this:

...and looks at only two of them – any two.

The player on the Dealer's left then turns over the card on the top of the pile. If it is lower than either of the two of his own cards which he looked at, he may swap it and throw down the one he was dealt to form a waste pile. The card he has just taken goes into the gap, face down.

The next player, and every one thereafter, has a choice; either he can turn a card over from the stack, or he can pick up the card from the top of the waste pile if he thinks it is better than any he already has. If a very good card comes up, a player might risk changing it for one of his two unseen cards. In this way he sometimes gets it wrong and ends up throwing out a King, which is very good news for the player whose turn it is next!

When a player thinks he has a good enough set of cards, he bangs on the table as he finishes his turn to end the game. Everyone else is allowed one more go, and then all the players must turn over their four cards and count up their scores. The player with the lowest score wins.

What if...?
You don't want another go at the end because you were thinking of banging on the table yourself?
You don't have to have it.

---

40 CARD GAMES

Card Call

Up to 10 players

There's no skill at all in this game, but it's a lot of fun if you don't take it too seriously!

How To Play

The Dealer deals all the cards one at a time to everyone, so that each player has the same number of cards; if there are any left over he places these face up in the middle of the table to form a waste pile. The players do not look at their cards but, in turn, starting with the player to the left of the Dealer, they lay a card on the waste pile (starting one if there isn't one already). But, before they do this, however, they must call out the suit they think it will be – clubs, hearts, spades or diamonds.

If they guess right they pick up all the cards in the pile, but keep them separate from the ones dealt to them. These cards are their winnings and at the end of the game the winner is the person with the most cards. The only ones they play with are those dealt to them at the start of the game.

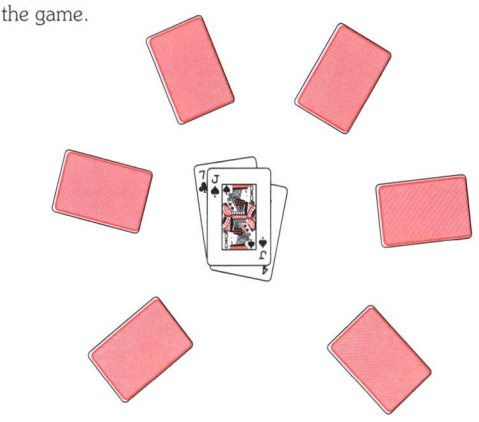

What if...?
Nobody wins the waste pile at the end of the game?
The cards are left unclaimed and not counted in anyone's final score.

CARD GAMES

Newmarket

2 – 10 players (it is more fun with lots of people).

This is a gambling game – but play with used matchsticks, buttons or Monopoly money so that no one ends up wishing they hadn't played because they lost all their pocket money!

Newmarket is a famous centre of horse racing and the idea of this game is to 'race' your cards to see who wins.

How To Play

You need two packs of cards, but you use only four from the second pack. These are the ten of hearts, the Jack of clubs, the Queen of diamonds and the King of spades. These are the racehorses, and they should be put face up in a square in the centre of the table.

Each player now places a matchstick on to one of these horses (he can choose which one for himself) and also places another matchstick into a central kitty. Everyone should start with the same amount of matchsticks.

The players now cut the pack to decide who is to be Dealer (it's the one who cuts the highest card – Ace is high). The Dealer deals all the cards out, face down, to the players, but deals two hands for himself. Don't worry if some players get more cards than others.

All the players pick up their cards and look at them. The Dealer, though, picks up only ONE of his sets of cards. If he likes what he sees, he keeps it. But if he thinks the cards are poor, he may swap it for the other set of cards in front of him. He's not allowed to swap it back again, though, if he finds that these are worse than the first ones! If he doesn't swap, the spare hand is offered to the player on his left, and if he doesn't want it, each player round the table in turn has a chance to swap their cards for it. If no one wants it, it is removed from the table. But anyone (other than the Dealer) who wants to swap must pay one more matchstick into the kitty as a fee for doing so, and must keep it once the swap has been made.

42 CARD GAMES

Now the racing can start! The player on the Dealer's left starts by putting down a card, face up, which may be of any suit, but which is the lowest card he holds in that suit. As he puts it down he calls out the name of it. For example, he might say, "four of diamonds!", and this starts the race; whoever has the five of diamonds lays it, calling out the name as he does so. The race carries on as far as possible, with a clear run through the six, seven, eight, nine, ten, Jack, Queen, King, to the Ace of diamonds. Because there is a spare hand, most races will never get as far as the Ace. When a run is blocked, the person who played the last card begins again with the lowest card he holds in a suit. There is only one rule about this; it has to be the opposite colour from the last race run, so if the player who won the last race holds none of that colour, the first player on his right who has such a card starts instead. And off everyone goes again.

Whenever a player lays a card which is the same as one of the horses in the centre of the table, he can pick up the matchsticks on that card!

The first player to get rid of all his cards wins all the matchsticks in the kitty. If you want to finish before this happens, keep the kitty intact for another day.

There are lots of different versions of this game, but if you learn to play it this way first you will be sure of the basic idea before you try adding any complicated extra rules.

What if...?
No one has any cards of the other colour from the one just played when a new race is due to start?
That's the end of the round and the cards have to be collected and dealt again!

CARD GAMES 43

Hearts

4 players only
In this game you try to lose all the time!

How To Play

The cards are shuffled and the Dealer deals out the cards, face down and one at a time, to each of the four players. One of these players must have a pencil and some paper, because you need to keep a score in this game.

Everyone should check that they have 13 cards each; this is important.

The player on the Dealer's left places a card in the middle of the table. It can be any card he likes. Then the other three players put down a card. Theirs must be of the same suit as the first card played; doing this is called 'following suit'. If anyone hasn't got a card in that suit, they can put down any other card. It is a good idea to use a heart when you can't follow suit in this game, as the idea is to lose all your hearts and all tricks containing them. (A trick is one round of play in which all the players played one card.) And the best hearts to play when you can't follow suit are the ones of high value, such as the picture cards and the Ace.

If you haven't got a heart, either, you can use any card.

The winner of the trick is the person who has played the highest card in the suit which started the round. And the winner of the game is the person who ends up with the fewest penalty points.

Here is how you score:
- **5 points for the Ace of hearts**
- **4 points for the King**
- **3 points for the Queen**
- **2 points for the Jack of hearts**
- **1 point for each of the other heart cards**

But if you win **ALL** the hearts your previous score is wiped out. This is called 'shooting the moon'. So don't get fed up if you win the first few tricks; see if you can win them all!

What if...?
Someone insists on calling this game Trumps, which is another name for it?

They shouldn't, because there aren't any trumps in this game, and it can lead people to think that in games which have trumps in them they are always hearts.

Ninety-Eight

As many players as you like can play, as long as you have one pack of cards for each four players. The object of this game is to find a loser, not a winner.

How To Play

Shuffle the cards – if there are lots of packs (and therefore too many to hold in your hands all at once) you might need to mix them all up on a table, then pick them up in batches to deal them out. Deal out three to each player. The rest of the cards are placed in a stack, face down on the table, and when any player lays a card, he picks up a replacement from the stack.

The player on the left of the Dealer starts by laying any card he likes from his hand and the other players do the same, in turn. Every time a card is laid, its face value is added to the value of those already laid, and the total shouted out by the player laying the card.

The value of the cards is as follows:

Aces = 1

Twos to Nines = face value

Jacks and Kings = 10

Queens = 0

Tens = minus 10

What everyone is trying to avoid is to be the person who lays the card which brings the score to 98 or more. If a player cannot help but do this when it comes to his turn, then he's the loser and the game is at an end.

What if...?
You have a hand with lots of tens and Queens in it?
That's a good hand! Hang on to them and try to get rid of your high-scoring cards as soon as you can.

Extras

A pack of cards can be used for things other than playing games. Try to build a house of cards – there is no way of doing this which will ensure that it doesn't immediately fall down (unless you cheat and use sticky tape, which ruins the cards). When you have lost patience with that, try out some of these card tricks...

The Flip Trick

Here's an easy card trick which should fool everyone.

The Trick

Tell your audience that you will show them an amazing thing – you will flip a card over in the pack without removing it first! Then before their eyes, shuffle the pack and, holding the pack out face down, invite someone to choose one from it. Tell them to look at it and replace it in the pack (which you are holding out to them).

Then put the cards down, tap the top of the pack with your finger, and go through the cards until you come to – hey presto! – their chosen card, facing upwards.

How It's Done

Before you start, prepare your pack by turning over the last card in the pack, so that the back is showing instead of the face. When you shuffle the cards, don't let your audience see that the last card is facing the other way, and don't let this card get shuffled, but keep it in its position at the end. When you hold out the pack for someone to pick a card, this turned card should be on the bottom, not the top, so that the card picked out is face down like the top one. While they are looking at their chosen card, smoothly turn the pack over in your hands, so that when they put it back, face down, it will in fact be the only one, apart from the top card, which is facing that way.

When you put the cards down to tap them, turn them over as you do so – and, of course, the turned card in the middle of the pack will be the chosen one. Don't let them see the other turned card at the end!

Which Row?

Amaze everyone by getting the right card every time!

How To Play

Use 21 cards only for this trick. Shuffle them and invite someone to choose a card from among them, look at it, and replace it in the pack. Then say that you will tell them which card it was, simply by dealing them out several times. First, deal them in three vertical rows of seven, and ask the person to tell you which row his card is in. Pick up one of the other rows, then pick up the row the chosen card is in, and put these seven cards on top of the other seven. Finally, pick up the last row and put those cards on top of the ones in your hand. The chosen card and the others in its row will now be in the centre of your pack.

Next, deal them out again, this time by dealing three cards next to each other, and then the next three on top of them, overlapping them slightly, and so on until you, once again, have three rows of seven cards. Ask which row the chosen one is in, then pick them up as before. Deal them once again in this way (as you did the second time) and when the person tells you which row contains his card, pick them up again in the same way.

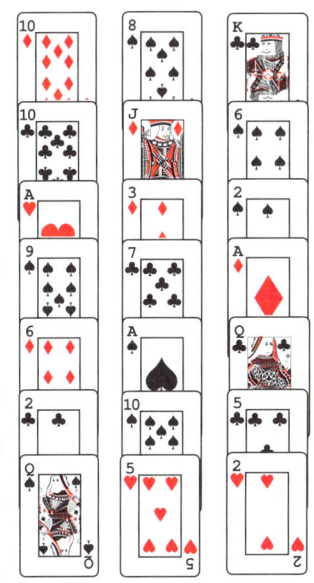

Now deal out ten cards in one pile, face down. Deal the eleventh card face up and it will be the chosen one!

There are no secret moves to make with this trick – it just works out that way!

CARD GAMES 47

I Can Read Your Mind!

Have you got the gift of the gab? You need to talk and talk just like a real fortune-teller while you work it!

The Trick

Take 20 cards from the pack and put the others aside – they are not needed. Place your 20 cards face down in pairs on the table. Then leave the room while someone from your audience chooses a pair, looks at them to see which cards they are, and then replaces them so that when you return you will not be able to guess which pair were looked at.

Pick them up at random (keeping the pairs together) and then lay them out on the table in front of you. Deal a row of five cards next to each other, with three more rows just like it under them, making a square. While you do this, chat about the weather, what you did on the way to school – anything; but whatever you do, *lay them down in the order shown on Plan 1, or the trick will not work.* Then ask them which row or rows their cards are in.

When they tell you, pick up and discard the cards in the other two or three rows. Then study the cards which remain. While you do this, stare very closely from time to time at the person who chose the cards, as if you really are trying to read his mind. Of course you aren't – you are merely playing for time while you remember in what order you laid them. For this reason you need to practise by yourself many times before you try this on anyone else. When you get to know this trick perfectly, you will see at once which cards go together, even though you laid them down in such a haphazard way.

For example, in each row there is one pair, side by side. In the first row, it is the first two cards. In the second row, it is cards 2 and 3. It is cards 3 and 4 in the third row and the last two cards in the fourth. So if you are told that both cards are in one row, you'll know they are next to each other – and which two they are will depend on which row it is.

If one card is in one row and the other in another, you know they aren't side by side. After that, you can easily work it out by remembering how you laid them. To help you see it easily for yourself, here are two plans; Plan 1, which tells you the order in which to lay them, and Plan 2, which shows you in symbols the way the pairs get broken up. Learn where they are and you should get it right every time.

When you know which cards are the chosen ones, chat away as you pick up the others around them. Say things like: "I feel that spades are unlucky here...these numbers are too low to be useful...the Kings are unlucky today..." and so on, removing cards as you speak, until at last the two chosen ones are the only ones on the table.

48 CARD GAMES